NATIVE NATIONS OF NORTH AMERICA

Nations of the
NORTHEAST COAST

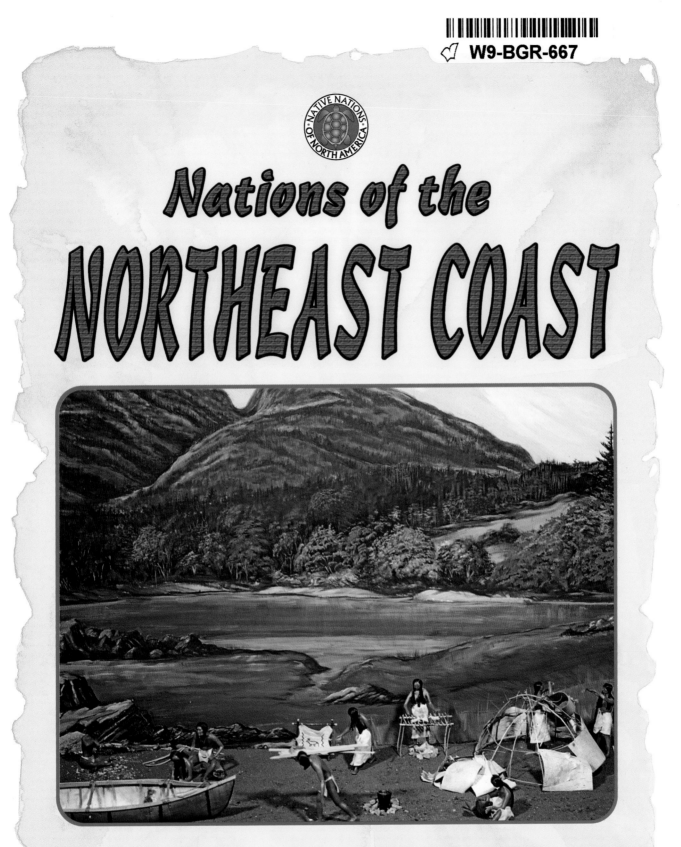

Molly Aloian & Bobbie Kalman

🌱 Crabtree Publishing Company

www.crabtreebooks.com

Nations of the Northeast Coast

Created by Bobbie Kalman

Dedicated by Katherine Berti
To my dearest grandparents, Stefan and Anna Kantor, with all of my love.

Editor-in-Chief
Bobbie Kalman

Writing team
Molly Aloian
Bobbie Kalman

Substantive editor
Kathryn Smithyman

Editors
Kelley MacAulay
Reagan Miller
Rebecca Sjonger

Design
Katherine Berti

Cover design
Katherine Berti
Samantha Crabtree

Production coordinator
Heather Fitzpatrick

Photo research
Crystal Sikkens

Consultants
Ron Welburn (Cherokee/Southeastern Algonquin), Professor of English,
    Director of Native American Indian Studies Certificate Program
    University of Massachusetts Amherst
Dr. Lisa Rankin, Associate Professor of Anthropology, Memorial University of Newfoundland

Illustrations
Barbara Bedell: pages 13, 15 (top), 18 (top), 21 (canoe, snowshoes on right)
Katherine Berti: border, page 4 (coast map)
Bonna Rouse: pages 4 (map of North America), 10 (clay pot), 11 (beans)
Margaret Amy Salter: back cover (background), title page (background), pages 5, 10 (background),
    11 (squash and corn), 17 (bottom), 21 (toboggan, snowshoes on left), 22 (right)

Photographs and reproductions
From the collection of the Abbe Museum, Bar Harbor, Maine:
    back cover (inset), title page (except background), pages 8, 17 (top)
© Cara Lee Blume/ Model: Javid Kshuxwe Ridgeway, Nanticoke Lenni-Lenape Tribe: page 30
© Canadian Museum of Civilization, Prehistoric Sea Mammal Hunting,
    Canada Visual History, Vol. 65, # 23: page 7
The Granger Collection, New York: page 28
Historical Artist Robert Griffing and Publisher, Paramount Press Inc: pages 15 (bottom), 24, 27
W. Langdon Kihn, National Geographic Image Collection: page 18 (bottom)
Illustrations by John T. Kraft, courtesy of Lenape Lifeways, Inc.: pages 12, 16, 20, 23
© Permission of Lazare & Parker: page 22 (left)
Photos by Mashantucket Pequot Museum & Research Center: pages 11, 14, 19
National Archives of Canada/C-000803: page 6
Courtesy, National Museum of the American Indian, Smithsonian Institution (19/8130): page 13
New Brunswick Museum, Saint John, N.B./W5943 (detail): page 25
© Permission of Lewis Parker: pages 9, 26
Judith Pearson: page 10
Artwork from PicturesNow.com: front cover
Courtesy of Pilgrim Hall Museum, Plymouth, Massachusetts: page 29
© Alan Syliboy: page 31
Other images by Corel and Digital Vision

Crabtree Publishing Company

www.crabtreebooks.com   1-800-387-7650

Copyright © **2006 CRABTREE PUBLISHING COMPANY.**
All rights reserved. No part of this publication may be
reproduced, stored in a retrieval system or be transmitted in
any form or by any means, electronic, mechanical, photocopying,
recording, or otherwise, without the prior written permission
of Crabtree Publishing Company. In Canada: We acknowledge
the financial support of the Government of Canada through
the Book Publishing Industry Development Program (BPIDP)
for our publishing activities.

Printed in the USA/032010/CG20100208

Cataloging-in-Publication Data
Aloian, Molly.
    Nations of the Northeast coast / Molly Aloian & Bobbie Kalman.
        p. cm. -- (Native nations of North America series)
    Includes index.
    ISBN-13: 978-0-7787-0386-0 (rlb)
    ISBN-10: 0-7787-0386-X (rlb)
    ISBN-13: 978-0-7787-0478-2 (pbk)
    ISBN-10: 0-7787-0478-5 (pbk)
    1. Indians of North America--Northeastern States--History--Juvenile literature.
    2. Indians of North America--Northeastern States--Social life and customs--
    Juvenile literature. 3. Indians of North America--Maritime Provinces--History--
    Juvenile literature. 4. Indians of North America--Maritime Provinces--Social life
    and customs--Juvenile literature.
    I. Kalman, Bobbie. II. Title. III. Native nations of North America.
    E78.E2A56 2006
    974.004'97--dc22
                                                                2005019988
                                                                LC

**Published in
the United States**

PMB 59051
350 Fifth Avenue,
59th Floor
New York, New York
10118

**Published
in Canada**

616 Welland Ave.,
St. Catharines, Ontario,
Canada
L2M 5V6

**Published in the
United Kingdom**

Maritime House
Basin Road North,
Hove
BN41 1WR
United Kingdom

**Published
in Australia**

386 Mt. Alexander Rd.,
Ascot Vale (Melbourne)
VIC 3032

Contents

The Northeast Coast

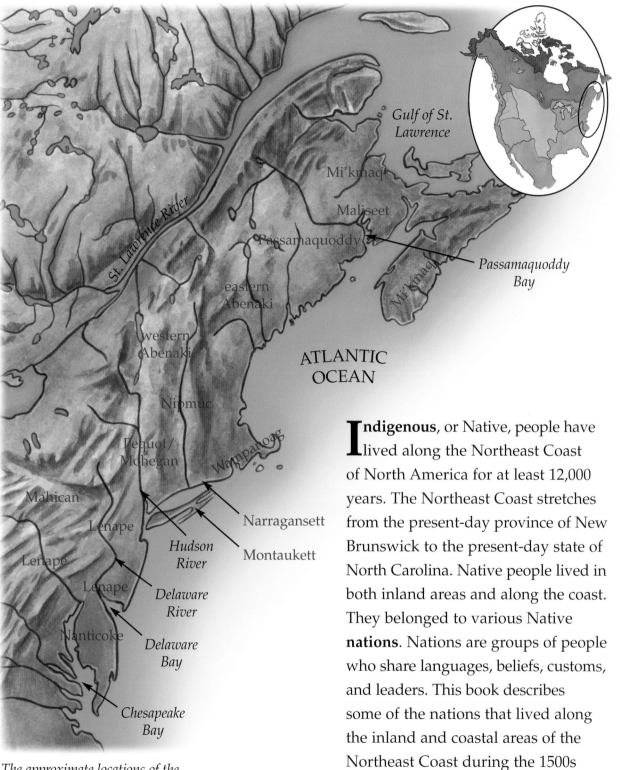

The approximate locations of the nations described in this book are shown on the map above.

Indigenous, or Native, people have lived along the Northeast Coast of North America for at least 12,000 years. The Northeast Coast stretches from the present-day province of New Brunswick to the present-day state of North Carolina. Native people lived in both inland areas and along the coast. They belonged to various Native **nations**. Nations are groups of people who share languages, beliefs, customs, and leaders. This book describes some of the nations that lived along the inland and coastal areas of the Northeast Coast during the 1500s and 1600s, when European explorers, settlers, and traders first arrived there.

4

Different territories

Each nation had a **territory**, or an area of land in which its people hunted, fished, planted crops, and gathered wild plants for food. The territories included the Atlantic Ocean, many lakes and rivers, and forests. The waterways and forests provided people with food and many **natural resources**, or useful materials found in nature. The people of some nations lived in permanent villages. Others lived in temporary camps made up of portable homes. They moved these temporary camps from place to place as the seasons changed.

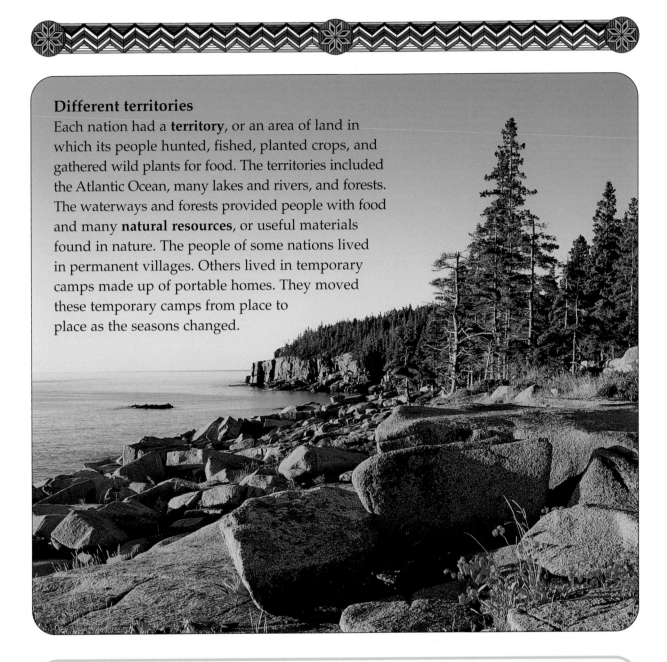

Different climates

The northern part of the Northeast Coast has a **climate** that is different from the climates in the central and southern parts of the coast. In the northern part, winters are cold and long, and summers are often warm and short. In the central and southern parts of the region, the winter weather is mild and the summers are hot and long.

Different languages

The people of most nations spoke different languages, but all the languages spoken in the region belonged to the Algonquian **language family**. A language family is made up of languages that are similar to one another. The people of some nations spoke the same language, but they spoke different **dialects**, or versions of the language. For example, the Maliseet and the Passamaquoddy spoke different dialects of the same Algonquian language.

Northern nations

Three nations that lived throughout the northern part of the Northeast Coast were the Mi'kmaq, the Passamaquoddy, and the Maliseet. The people of each nation lived in large villages during spring and summer. They set up smaller hunting camps in different territories during the cold winter months.

The Mi'kmaq

Before and during the 1500s, the Mi'kmaq nation may have had more than 35,000 members. The Mi'kmaq may have called themselves "L'nu'k," which meant "human" or "people" in their language. They called their territory "Megumaage." It was located in the present-day provinces of Nova Scotia, New Brunswick, Prince Edward Island, and Quebec. Mi'kmaq territory included parts of the Atlantic Ocean and its shores, dense forests, and many lakes and rivers. The Mi'kmaq were skilled hunters and fishers. They hunted elk and bears in the forests and fished for smelt and herring in the lakes and rivers. They also gathered shellfish and hunted seals and other ocean animals.

The Passamaquoddy

Passamaquoddy territory was located along the coasts of present-day New Brunswick and Maine, near Passamaquoddy Bay and the St. Croix River. The people hunted some inland animals, such as moose, but they mainly hunted and gathered foods from the ocean. The men were skilled fishers. The name "Passamaquoddy" means "those who pursue the pollock" or "pollock-spearing place." Passamaquoddy men fished for pollock, salmon, bass, and other fish. The women gathered lobsters and other shellfish from the ocean.

The Maliseet

The name "Maliseet" is most likely a Mi'kmaq word, which means "lazy speakers" or "broken talkers." The Maliseet lived in present-day New Brunswick and in northeastern Maine. Some historians believe that the Maliseet and the Passamaquoddy are closely related nations and that they may have once been one nation. In the early 1600s, thousands of Maliseet and Passamaquoddy people lived in the area. Maliseet men hunted mainly inland animals, including moose, deers, and bears.

The Passamaquoddy hunted seals and other ocean animals using **harpoons**, *or long spears. Groups of men in birchbark canoes worked together to hunt the animals.*

The eastern and western Abenaki

Many other nations lived in the northern parts of the Northeast Coast. These nations included the Kennebec, the Pigwacket, the Penobscot, the Arosaguntacook, the Penacook, the Sokoki, the Winnipesaukee, and the Mississquoi. Many historians group the Kennebec, the Pigwacket, the Penobscot, and the Arosaguntacook together and refer to them as the "eastern Abenaki." The eastern Abenaki spoke the same dialect of the Abenaki language. Each nation had traditional territory in present-day Maine. The name "Abenaki" means "dawn-land people" or "easterners."

Historians often group the Penacook, the Sokoki, the Winnipesaukee, and the Mississquoi together and refer to them as the "western Abenaki." The villages of the western Abenaki were farther west than the villages of the eastern Abenaki. Western Abenaki territories were in present-day New Hampshire and Vermont. The people spoke similar dialects of the Abenaki language. During the early 1500s, there may have been more than 40,000 eastern and western Abenaki people. Both the eastern and western Abenaki called themselves "Wabanaki."

The Abenaki were called "dawn-land people" because they lived along the east coast, where the sun rises each morning at dawn.

Abenaki territories

Eastern and western Abenaki territories were made up of forests, meadows, rivers, and other waterways. The people built their villages near meadows and waterways so they could hunt, fish, and travel easily by canoe. They found everything they needed to survive in their territories. They caught salmon, eel, and smelt in the waterways using hooks, nets, spears, and harpoons. Abenaki men hunted animals, such as caribou, deer, and beaver, in the meadows.

Women made clothing, including leggings, fur robes, belts, skirts, blouses, and moccasins, out of animal **hides**, or skins. They also gathered plant foods, such as berries, nuts, cherries, and other fruits, from the meadows. Some western Abenaki women grew crops, including corn, beans, squash, and tobacco. The soil in many eastern Abenaki territories was not good for growing crops, however. In spring, many eastern Abenaki women gathered shellfish and other foods from the ocean.

Central nations

Like all nations, the Wampanoag made everyday items, such as this clay pot, which were both beautiful and useful.

The Wampanoag, the Narragansett, the Nipmuc, and the Pequot/Mohegan are four nations that lived in the central part of the Northeast Coast. Their territories were located both along the coast and inland. The Montaukett are related to these people. The Montaukett lived in the eastern part of present-day Long Island.

The Wampanoag

Wampanoag territory was located in present-day eastern Rhode Island and in southeastern Massachusetts. In the 1600s, there were about 12,000 Wampanoag people living in this area. The Wampanoag were once called "Pokanoket," which was the name of their main village. During the early 1600s, there were at least 40 Wampanoag villages.

The Narragansett

Many historians believe that the Narragansett nation has lived in North America longer than most other Native nations. The name "Narragansett" means "people of the small point." The Narragansett had territories throughout most of present-day Rhode Island. They believed in a great Creator called Cautantowwit. According to the Narragansett legend, Cautantowwit sent a crow to their fields with the first seeds of corn and beans, on which the Narragansett relied for food. In the 1600s, the Narragansett nation was made up of approximately 10,000 people.

This wooden statue was carved by an artist named Peter Toth. The statue is called Enishkeetompauog Narragansett. It is named after a Narragansett **chief**, *or leader, and is over 20 feet (6.1 m) tall.*

The Nipmuc

Nipmuc territory was located in present-day Massachusetts, Connecticut, and Rhode Island. The name "Nipmuc" comes from the Algonquian word "nipmaug," which means "freshwater people." Nipmuc territory was not as close to the Atlantic Ocean as were the territories of other coastal nations. Instead of fishing in the ocean, the Nipmuc fished in inland freshwater lakes and rivers. They also grew crops of corn, beans, and squash. In the 1500s, there may have been more than 15,000 members of the Nipmuc nation.

The Pequot/Mohegan

The Mohegan were once part of the Pequot nation. In the early 1500s, the Pequot left their territory in the lower part of present-day New York. They traveled to an area of land near the Thames River in the southeastern part of present-day Connecticut. The Pequot are known as "fox people." In the early 1600s, a Pequot chief named Uncas left the village with a group of his followers. Uncas and his followers established a new village near the Connecticut River. They began calling themselves "Mohegan," which means "wolf people." Before the nation split in the early 1600s, there were more than 6,000 members of the Pequot nation.

The Pequot made dugout canoes that were between ten and fourteen feet (3-4.3 m) long and carried between two and four people. The Pequot used their canoes to travel and fish throughout their territory.

Southern nations

The Lenape, the Nanticoke, and the Mahican were three nations that lived throughout the southern parts of the Northeast Coast.

The Lenape

The name "Lenape" or "Lenni Lenape" means "human beings" or "real people." Lenape territory stretched from the northern part of present-day Chesapeake Bay to present-day New York, and included the western half of Long Island. Other nations in the area called the Lenape nation "grandfather" because they believed that the Lenape territory was the original homeland of many of the people in the region. In the 1600s, the Lenape nation may have had as many as 20,000 members, who lived in 30 to 40 villages. Lenape men hunted white-tailed deer in the woods near their territory. Like many other animals, white-tailed deer were of great importance to the Lenape. The people used the meat for food and made clothing, blankets, and other items from the hides. The people also crafted tools and weapons out of deer bones and antlers.

In addition to deer, the Lenape hunted birds. People used nets made of plant fibers to capture the birds.

The Nanticoke

The Nanticoke, as well as the Piscataway, the Choptank, and the Assateague, thought of themselves as "brother nations" or sub-nations of the Lenape nation. These nations lived in neighboring territories and spoke the same language. Nanticoke territory was on the **peninsula** between Delaware Bay and Chesapeake Bay. The people fished in the bays, along the coast, and in the rivers nearby. Nanticoke men cleared areas of land on which the women planted crops, including corn, beans, and pumpkins. Women grew several varieties of corn.

*Corn was used to make breads, soups, and other foods. Corn had to be prepared before it could be eaten, however. Women scraped the kernels off the ears of corn, shown left, and then mashed the corn in **mortars** made of hollowed-out logs, shown right.*

The Mahican

The Mahican (Mohican) called themselves "Muhhconneok," which means "people of the waters that are never still." Mahican territory was located in the eastern part of present-day New York and in the western part of present-day Vermont, Massachusetts, and Connecticut. The Mahican had territory on both sides of the Hudson River. During the 1600s, there were about 8,000 members of the Mahican nation. The name of their main village was Schodac. Like many other nations in the area, Mahican women grew corn, beans, squash, and sunflowers. Men often helped the women gather the harvests.

The Mahican carved spoons and other utensils out of wood. A face has been carved at the end of this spoon handle.

Families, bands, and clans

The people of the Northeast Coast lived with their **extended families**, which include grandparents, parents, children, aunts, uncles, and cousins. Children were taught how to help their parents with daily chores. Young girls watched their mothers and aunts to learn how to plant and tend crops, gather and cook foods, and make clothing. Boys watched their fathers and uncles to learn how to make weapons and how to hunt and fish. Children learned that the jobs of women and men were equally important. Children also learned to respect the land and to be grateful for everything that they took from it.

Bands

The people of most nations along the Northeast Coast belonged to **bands**. Bands were groups of people who lived together in villages and had their own customs and traditions. Many bands also had their own Native names and their own territories. Some bands were made up of groups of families that gathered together at certain times during the year. Bands usually came together in spring. Most bands contained between 50 and several hundred people.

This young boy is learning how to make arrows by watching an older member of his family.

Clans

Many people also belonged to **clans**. A clan is a group of people who believe that they share an **ancestor**. The ancestor is represented by an animal spirit, such as a wolf or a bear. Most clans were **matrilineal**. In a matrilineal clan, children became a part of their mother's clan as soon as they were born.

Chiefs

Each village had one or more chiefs. Most chiefs were men, but some villages had female chiefs. Many chiefs led entire villages, but some chiefs ruled over only their clans. Some chiefs inherited their positions from their fathers. Others inherited their positions from their mothers. Certain men became chiefs if they proved themselves to be strong leaders or skilled hunters.

A chief's responsibilities

Chiefs were often responsible for leading hunting trips, offering advice to people, and **mediating**. Mediating is settling disagreements between people in a village or between people from different villages. Chiefs were careful to listen to the points of view of all the people who were involved in a disagreement. Chiefs, along with elder members of the village and other respected individuals, often formed **councils**. The councils came together to make important decisions for the village, such as going to war with other nations.

Village life

The people of the Northeast Coast lived in villages of various sizes, which were usually located near waterways. Most villages were made up of about ten homes, but some contained up to 30 homes. People lived in two types of homes—large rectangular longhouses and domed or cone-shaped wigwams. The people of some nations had both kinds of dwellings in their villages.

Permanent villages

The people of some nations, including the Lenape, lived for most of the year in large permanent villages and moved to temporary camps at different times of the year to gather food, to hunt, and to fish. As the seasons changed, different foods were available in different places. For example, in summer, many women gathered wild grapes, berries, and other fruits from the forests near their large summer villages. In fall and winter, many nations left their summer villages and moved to different parts of their territories, where they set up small winter hunting camps. While at their winter camps, men hunted moose, bears, elk, and other animals to feed the people in their camp.

Most of the nations that had permanent villages lived in longhouses, as shown above. Longhouses had arched roofs that were covered in sheets of bark. These homes were often large enough to hold several families.

Temporary camps

Other nations did not have large permanent villages. Instead, families moved to new camps each time the seasons changed. The people returned to the same locations year after year, however. During spring, they often traveled to fishing spots. They also gathered shellfish and other ocean foods during this time. They planted crops in spring or summer and collected the harvests in fall. Spring and summer villages were often made up of several families. When winter arrived, the families split up and moved to their traditional winter hunting camps, where they lived and hunted during the cold months. Winter camps were smaller than summer camps because the harsh weather often made it difficult to feed large groups of people.

Winter camps were usually made up of one or more wigwams, which were set up near waterways. The people were sure to choose sites where there was plenty of firewood.

Portable homes

Many of the nations that moved with the seasons, including the Mi'kmaq and the Narragansett, lived in wigwams. Wigwams were not as sturdy as were longhouses, but they could be transported easily from place to place. The wooden frames, along with the grass and birchbark mats, could be taken down easily, carried to new locations, and set up again.

Finding and growing foods

The people of the Northeast Coast knew how to find, grow, and prepare the foods they needed to survive, and always gave thanks for them. Men were skilled hunters and fishers, and women knew where to find different plant foods and how to care for and harvest crops.

To attract male moose, Mi'kmaq hunters imitated the sounds of female moose by making calls through cones of rolled birch bark, shown above. When a male moose that was looking for a female moose came into view, the hunters shot it.

Hunting and fishing

Men hunted seals, porpoises, caribou, deer, elk, raccoons, rabbits, bears, beavers, and other animals with bows and arrows, spears, and traps. They used nets, bone fishhooks, and **weirs** to catch fish. Women often dried, roasted, or smoked the fish and meat before it was eaten.

People were always careful to take only what they needed from nature. They did not kill more animals or gather more plants than the people of their villages were able to use.

18

Gathering foods

Women gathered a wide variety of foods from the forests and from specific areas of the coast. They gathered berries, nuts, roots, mushrooms, wild cherries, and other fruits from the meadows and forests. They traveled to the coast or to nearby islands to collect shellfish such as crabs, mussels, and clams from the shores.

Growing crops

The people of many nations cleared areas of land for crops by setting small fires that burned away trees, shrubs, and grasses in the area. After they cleared the land, they planted crops of beans, squash, sunflowers, tobacco, and several types of corn. People usually planted crops in early spring or summer and harvested them in late summer or early fall. Women planted the seeds and looked after the fields. The crops were planted close to the villages, so women could easily look after them and collect the harvests. In some nations, men were responsible for growing the tobacco crops.

Before planting seeds, women turned and loosened the soil with tools made of bones, stones, shells, and wood.

Collecting sap

In spring, the people of some nations collected **sap** from maple and birch trees. Sap is a sweet liquid that flows through trees and other plants. To collect sap, people hammered wooden spouts into tree trunks. Sap dripped out of the spouts and into birchbark containers. Women then boiled the sap and made it into syrup and sugar, which were added to various foods. The sugar added flavor to the foods and prevented them from spoiling.

Traveling from place to place

The Native people of the Northeast Coast traveled on foot year-round. They also traveled on the ocean, the lakes, the rivers, and the other waterways near their territories using different types of boats. The people of some nations built large dugout canoes that could travel on rough ocean waters. Others built birchbark canoes that were used for traveling on calm, smooth waterways. Some of these waterways led to traditional fishing, gathering, or hunting spots. Other waterways led to the villages of neighboring nations.

People visited their neighbors for the purpose of trading goods. The canoes were used to transport goods and people.

Traveling in winter

In winter, many waterways froze over and snow piled up on the ground. During this time of the year, the Native people of some nations, including the Maliseet, strapped on snowshoes, which kept them from sinking into deep snow as they walked from place to place. The people of some nations also used toboggans to transport goods from one place to another.

These Lenape men are making a dugout canoe. It often took several days to complete a canoe.

Carefully crafted canoes

Men constructed birchbark and dugout canoes out of trees. To make a birchbark canoe, they created a frame out of **saplings**, or young trees, and covered it with layers of bark from birch trees. The people of some nations covered the frames with moose hides or caribou hides instead of birch bark. When the canoes were not being used, the hides were placed on wigwams or other shelters. To make a dugout canoe, men hollowed out large logs with tools and **charred**, or burned, the surface of the wood. The soft burnt wood was then scraped out of the logs to make room for people and goods.

Birchbark canoes, such as the one shown above, were watertight and lightweight. Dugout canoes were also watertight, but they were heavier than birchbark canoes.

Toboggans

Some people used toboggans to transport items over snow-covered ground. Toboggans were made out of thin wooden boards that curled upward at the front ends. They could be loaded with food, furs, tools, wood, or other items and dragged from place to place with ropes made of plant materials.

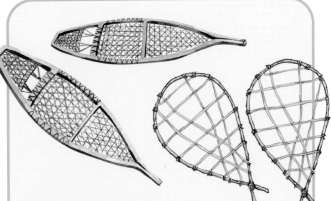

Snowshoes

Snowshoes are round or oval wooden frames with strips of leather woven across them. People attached snowshoes to their feet to help them walk over deep snow. Snowshoes also helped keep feet dry. Some nations made snowshoes that were slightly pointed at the front and back. The snowshoes of other nations were rounded at the front and pointed at the back.

Trade among nations

The Northeast Coast nations traded foods, goods, and other natural resources with one another throughout the year, but they traded more often during the summer. Most trading took place among nations that lived in neighboring territories. Different nations had different resources in their territories. The people traded these resources for items that they wanted or needed from other territories.

In the middle

Members of some nations, including people from the Mi'kmaq nation in the northern part of the region and people from the Mahican nation in the southern part of the region, acted as **intermediaries** between nations that traded goods with one another. An intermediary is a person who mediates between two or more people. Having intermediaries helped ensure that all trades made between people were fair. For example, the Mi'kmaq were often intermediaries between the nations that were mainly hunters in the northern region and the nations that were farmers in the southern region. The intermediaries helped establish trade agreements.

Both men and women prepared goods for trade, but men often traveled to different places to trade items with people from other nations.

Goods for trade

Some people traded furs, shells, and items made out of birch bark in exchange for items they did not make themselves, such as carved stone and wooden pipes. Other people traded certain foods or resources, such as chestnuts and seal oil, for foods they wanted or needed, such as corn. Some people went on trade expeditions that were far from their territories, but most trading took place between nations that lived close to one another.

Gifts of wampum

Certain nations harvested the shells of **quahogs**, which are a type of clam. People used quahog shells to make **wampum**. Wampum were small, **cylindrical** beads made from polished shells. When strung together to make belts or strings, the beads represented important events and told stories about the nations. Traditionally, people gave gifts of wampum to large, powerful nations.

Summer was the busiest trading season for the Lenape, shown above. The Lenape traded furs and other goods with other nations and acquired grass mats, baskets, and round-bottomed pots.

Europeans arrive

The first European explorers arrived along the Northeast Coast in the early 1500s. The eastern and western Abenaki and the Mi'kmaq were probably the first nations along the coast to have had contact with the Europeans. In 1524, members of the eastern and western Abenaki nations met an Italian explorer named Giovanni da Verrazano. Around the same time, the Mi'kmaq met a French explorer named Jacques Cartier, who arrived along the St. Lawrence River while looking for a passage to the west. The eastern and western Abenaki and the Mi'kmaq began trading animal hides and furs for knives and other iron goods that were made by Europeans. In 1604, another French explorer named Samuel de Champlain visited several Abenaki villages in order to trade. By the early 1600s, many nations, including the Maliseet, the Lenape, and the Mahican were trading regularly with Europeans. They traded animal furs and other items for European goods such as iron nails, kettles, knives, and cloth. Some nations acted as intermediaries between European traders and Native traders.

Europeans supplied Native people with metal weapons, including guns.

Changed lives

Contact with Europeans completely changed the lives of all Native people. The changes were not for the better, however. Native people began using European goods in their everyday lives and relied on their traditional tools less and less. They started using metal fishing hooks to catch fish and used iron kettles to boil water. Eventually, tensions and conflicts grew between the traders of certain nations because they were competing to trade goods with the French and other Europeans.

Diseases

Many Europeans carried diseases, such as smallpox and typhus, with which Native people had never before come in contact. The Native people did not have any natural defenses against these diseases. As a result, thousands of Native people became sick and died shortly after meeting European people and using their goods, such as blankets. By the mid 1600s, some nations were completely wiped out by **epidemics** of **smallpox** and **typhus**. An epidemic is an outbreak of a disease that quickly spreads from person to person.

The fur trade

By the mid to late 1600s, many nations along the coast were involved in the **fur trade** with French, English, and other European traders. Fur traders recognized the skills of Native hunters and encouraged them to trap as many animals, especially beavers, as they could. Beaver pelts were sold for a lot of money in Europe, where they were made into hats.

The demand for furs

As the demand for furs continued to grow in Europe, European traders wanted more and more animal furs. Some Europeans trapped the animals themselves. They moved to Native territories and forced the Native people off their lands. Other Europeans relied on Native people to trap large numbers of beavers and other animals. Many of the nations that lived along the coast began spending more time inland, where more animals lived. In order to remain living in their traditional territories, Native men began spending most of their time hunting and trapping animals and trading animal furs.

Eventually, Europeans claimed Native lands for themselves and began establishing trading posts on the lands. Many Native people continued to trade with Europeans because they felt they had no choice.

Native confederacies

Before Europeans arrived in the Northeast region, five nations that lived to the west of the coast formed a powerful **confederacy**, called the Haudenosaunee Confederacy. A confederacy is an association of two or more nations that join together to achieve common goals. The Haudenosaunee Confederacy included the Mohawk, Seneca, Oneida, Onondaga, and Cayuga nations. During the early 1600s, the nations in the Haudenosaunee Confederacy formed **alliances**, or partnerships, with the English. Together, the Haudenosaunee and the English fought the French for control of Native lands along the coast and inland, as well as for control of the fur trade. In the mid 1600s, the Passamaquoddy, the eastern and western Abenaki, the Mi'kmaq, the Maliseet, and several of the other nations that lived along the Northeast Coast joined together and formed the Wabanaki Confederacy. They formed this confederacy in order to protect themselves and their lands from the English and from the Haudenosaunee nations. Other nations, including the Mahican and the Wampanoag, also formed confederacies to protect themselves and their traditional territories. The Mahican Confederacy included the Mahican, the Housatonic, the Wappinger, and several other nations. The Wampanoag Confederacy included the Wampanoag, the Nauset, the Sakonnet, and various other nations.

When European explorers arrived in present-day New York, they offered the Mohawk people guns in exchange for furs and other items. The Mohawk used these weapons to drive the Mahican out of their territory.

Conflicts and change

This painting shows an English explorer named Roger Williams landing in Narragansett territory. He claimed the land as English territory. Today, the land is the present-day state of Rhode Island.

Additional conflicts arose between the Native people and Europeans, as the Europeans took over more Native lands during the 1600s. Thousands of Native people died trying to protect their territories. Many people from the Pequot nation died during the Pequot War in 1637. Hundreds of Narragansett warriors died in 1675, during a battle known today as the Great Swamp Fight. One year later, during King Philip's War, hundreds of Nipmuc, Narragansett, and Wampanoag people were killed. These wars, and the wars that followed them, had devastating effects on the populations of many Native nations.

Caught in the middle

Between 1754 and 1763, the British and the French fought more wars to gain control over Native lands and the natural resources they contained. The British wanted to claim Native territories so they could establish **colonies**. The French wanted to claim Native territories so they could control the fur trade in the region. Several Native nations along the coast and inland were caught in the middle of these wars. Nations throughout the Northeast Coast and in neighboring territories felt pressure to establish alliances with either the French or the British in order to protect their homelands from being taken. The people of some nations fought alongside the French in order to defeat the British. The people of other nations fought alongside the British. Most Native people fought in the wars because they believed that the Europeans would share the land once the wars had ended. The British eventually defeated the French in 1763, but they claimed all the land for themselves. Many Native people were forced to leave their homes and villages.

Forced to change

After the **American Revolution** ended in 1783, some Native land was still controlled by the British, but the rest was controlled by Americans. Many Native peoples were encouraged give up their cultures and their traditional ways of life and adopt European ways of life. As they had been doing for years, Catholic **missionaries** tried to convince Native people to give up their traditional religious beliefs and accept the Catholic religion. The missionaries built **missions**, or churches, in Native territories. The British and American governments continued to take control of the land and all its natural resources, so Native people could no longer hunt, fish, or gather foods.

Eventually, the American government began building farms, roads, bridges, and mills. They also established logging companies in Native territories.

Signing treaties

Many Native nations were forced to sign agreements called **treaties**, which established certain areas of land where Native people could live. These lands are known as **reservations** in the United States and **reserves** in Canada. Few reservations or reserves were on traditional Native territories, however. While living on the reservations and reserves, Native people felt even more pressure to give up their languages, cultures, and traditional beliefs.

The nations today

This picture was taken at a Nanticoke powwow in 2004. The powwow featured traditional dancing and drumming.

Today, thousands of **descendants** of the nations that lived along the Northeast Coast live in the United States and Canada. Some Native people live on reservations or reserves, and others live in non-Native communities. Although their lifestyles are similar to those of other Americans and Canadians, Native people still honor and celebrate their cultures as they did thousands of years ago.

Coming together

Many nations continue to hold traditional dances, festivals, feasts, and ceremonies during certain times of the year. Other nations have elected chiefs and other council members who act as leaders within their Native communities. The people of many nations work hard to bring together the people of their nations who are living in different communities. For example, a modern version of the Delaware Nation Grand Council of North America works to bring together various groups of the Lenape people. By coming together, the Lenape can maintain their relationships with one another and gather together for important cultural events.

Preserving languages

Some nations, such as the Passamaquoddy, are trying to preserve their languages. They are working to have the languages taught in public schools. The University of New Brunswick in New Brunswick, Canada is creating an online Maliseet-Passamaquoddy dictionary in order to preserve the languages of these nations and ensure that they are not lost. The dictionary includes over 8,000 entries and many more will be added in the future. Many Mi'kmaq people continue to speak their Native languages, as well.

Traditional arts

Many of today's Native artists create the same types of items as those made by their ancestors. Some Mi'kmaq and Maliseet basketmakers continue to make baskets in the traditional way, using birch bark. Certain Wampanoag artists make clay pots, including cooking pots and ceremonial pots, using traditional materials and shapes. By making these items, the artists honor their ancestors and preserve their cultures and traditions. The descendants of the people of the Northeast Coast are extremely proud of their **heritage**.

This print, entitled "Family," was made by a modern Mi'kmaq artist named Alan Syliboy. It shows a man, a woman, and a child holding hands and emphasizes the connection the artist feels with his ancestors.

Glossary

Note: Boldfaced words that are not defined in the book may not appear in the glossary.

American Revolution The war between the American colonies and Great Britain (1775-1783), which led to the formation of the United States

ancestor An ancient relative or spirit animal from whom or from which someone is believed to have descended

climate The long-term weather conditions in an area, including temperature, rainfall, and wind

colony An area of land ruled by a faraway country

council A group of people called together to give advice, discuss problems, and make decisions

cylindrical A solid or hollow object that is round on all sides

descendant A person who comes from a particular ancestor or group of ancestors

fur trade A system of trade in which items were exchanged for animal furs

heritage The history, traditions, and culture associated with one's ancestors

intermediary A person who tries to bring about an agreement between two or more groups of people

matrilineal Describing a type of kinship in which a person descends from his or her mother or mother's family line

missionary A religious person who tries to convert others to his or her religion

peninsula An area of land that extends into a body of water

smallpox A deadly disease, which causes a high fever, an achy body, and blisters on a person's body

typus A disease, which causes a high fever and a headache

weir A fence that is placed in a waterway to catch fish

Index